Acceptance and Commitment Therapy Journal

D1641493

ACCEPTANCE and COMMITMENT THERAPY journal

Prompts and Techniques to Practice
Acceptance While Building the Life You Want

Josie Valderrama, PsyD

ROCKRIDGE
PRESS

For general information on our other products and services or to obtain technical support, please contact our Customer Care Department within the United States at (866) 744-2665, or outside the United States at (510) 253-0500.

Rockridge Press publishes its books in a variety of electronic and print formats. Some content that appears in print may not be available in electronic books, and vice versa.

Interior and Cover Designer: Regina Stadnik
Art Producer: Alyssa Williams
Editor: Olivia Bartz
Production Editor: Caroline Flanagan
Production Manager: Holly Haydash

Author photo courtesy of Karaminder Ghuman

Paperback ISBN: 978-1-63878-746-4
eBook ISBN: 978-1-68539-130-0
R0

This journal belongs to:

_____

CONTENTS

INTRODUCTION

Welcome! I'm Dr. Josie Valderrama, and I am so pleased to embark on this journey with you. Years before I became a psychologist, I struggled to feel at peace. It often felt like there was a war going on in my head, and I was at a loss as to how to make things better. Thankfully, mindfulness practice, self-help books, and a ton of trial and error put me on the path to wellness.

When I discovered acceptance and commitment therapy (ACT) more than a decade ago, I immediately sensed its massive potential to liberate people from suffering. Since then, through my work with clients, I have seen how ACT changes lives for the better. With its melding of mindfulness and cognitive behavioral techniques, ACT is an incredibly effective tool, and I am excited to share its power with you.

Please keep in mind, this book is not a replacement for therapy, medication, or medical treatment. If feelings of depression or anxiety have been ongoing or debilitating, please consult with a medical professional. There is never shame in seeking help or treatment.

Think of this book as a trusty companion as you move through life transitions, emotional upheaval, and everyday challenges. Let the time you spend here be a symbol of your compassionate intention for healing and growth. My heartfelt wish is that this exploration fosters greater well-being and purpose in your life.

How to Use This Book

This book is formatted as a guided journal. There are six sections, each focused on one of the core processes at the foundation of the ACT approach. In each section, you will find prompts, affirmations, exercises, and practices that will help you, not only intellectually understand the core concept, but also directly connect with it as a lived process.

ACT core processes stand on their own as important principles for elevating quality of life. At the same time, they are interrelated and together form the basis for psychological flexibility. Please read the descriptions at the beginning of each section before proceeding.

Though there's no official order to follow in ACT, it can be helpful to go through this book in order, as explanations build on one another. Experiment with incorporating this journal into your routine, or turn to it when it calls to you. There's no wrong way to approach the work.

A BRIEF INTRODUCTION TO ACCEPTANCE AND COMMITMENT THERAPY

ACT is a science-based therapy and research orientation that aims to strengthen psychological flexibility. Psychological flexibility is the ability to be in a state of presence through life's highs and lows while acting based on your chosen values. In contrast to most other therapies, the goal of ACT is not to try to get rid of symptoms. Instead, the focus is on mindful acceptance, identifying your deepest values, and moving toward greater meaning.

At the crux of ACT is paradox. By not fighting reality, you can get the change you wanted all along. The goal of ACT is to help you accept what is while also committing to take things to the next level.

Study after study has proven ACT's effectiveness in helping with a range of mental health issues. But ACT is not just for those who are struggling. Anyone can benefit from its formula for personal liberation.

ACT is founded on six core principles, each of which has its own chapter in this book. These principles are referred to as processes, reflecting ACT's focus on continuous progression and actionable goals. Cognitive defusion cultivates healthy nonattachment from your thoughts. Acceptance is about compassionately being with what is. Contacting the present moment deepens awareness of the here and now. The observing self steps outside of and observes the part of you that thinks, feels, and acts. Values exploration uncovers motivation and meaning. Committed action puts values into practice for real world results. Each core process is described further in its own chapter.

Cognitive Defusion: Taking Space from Your Thoughts

When you are cognitively fused, you are stuck inside your thoughts and forced to identify with their perspective. Cognitive defusion frees you to clearly see your thoughts by separating your thoughts from your sense of self. It may sound strange at first to realize that you are not your thoughts. But without this critical lens, you may tend to assume that your thoughts are unquestionable reality. Without cognitive defusion you can get stuck in self-limiting beliefs and unhelpful thinking. So, it is beneficial to learn to defuse from your thoughts by *seeing* them rather than *being* them.

On a practical level, cognitive defusion may show up in a variety of ways. It can involve realizing that an inner critic is perpetually running in the background or that you tend to get annoyed by a particular thought that always precedes conflicts with your partner. It can also be the realization that a longtime opinion you hold feels outdated and untrue. Really, it's any time that you catch yourself in the act of unhelpful autopilot thinking.

Thoughts are simply words, images, and associations. I am so much more than my thoughts.

One way to cognitively defuse is to frame your thoughts by adding container phrases like "I'm having the thought that . . ." Try rephrasing your most common unhelpful thoughts in this way. Then reflect for a few moments and note your observations. Here's an example: "I'm noticing I'm having the thought that I'm not good enough."

_____

_____

_____

_____

Defuse through silliness! Turn challenging thoughts into jingles playing in the background, annoying but harmless. Imagine them said in comical cartoon voices or say the thoughts aloud in exaggerated slow motion. It's not about making fun of the thought but simply gaining a different perspective. How do you feel about the thoughts now?

_____

_____

_____

_____

You can defuse by externalizing thoughts onto the page. Write a list of your "repeat offender" thoughts. This exercise can be daunting, so keep breathing and be compassionate with yourself. When you're done, read over what you wrote. Note any shifts in your perspective or other reactions.

_____

_____

_____

_____

_____

_____

_____

_____

_____

_____

_____

_____

In poker, a tell is when body language shifts in response to a change in the player's fortunes. When you are fused with unpleasant thoughts, you tend to have tells. Maybe you start scratching your arm or suddenly feel overheated. Consider your "tells." What thoughts are associated with them?

_____

_____

_____

_____

_____

_____

_____

_____

_____

_____

_____

_____

_____

Flipping the Script: Cognitive Defusion

List some instances where you found yourself in a fused state. Then write out an alternative perspective through the lens of cognitive defusion. Remember that when you get fused, you are trapped in the viewpoint of your thoughts. When you achieve defusion, you are able to clearly see your thoughts from the outside looking in.

FUSION	DEFUSION
Example: *When I went to the party, I decided that there was something wrong with everyone there.*	**Example:** *Social anxiety clouded my perception of others. I look at my thoughts with compassion and a healthy dose of skepticism.*
Example: *After reading the job description, I didn't apply because I knew I'd be rejected.*	**Example:** *I was having depressive thoughts that underestimated my potential.*

When you're really stuck on a particular thought, it can be helpful to adopt a different perspective. First see yourself outside yourself. Then zoom farther out so you are looking down at yourself from the sky. Zoom into outer space, looking at the planet. Then quickly zoom back, reversing the stages. What do you notice?

_____

_____

_____

_____

Research has shown that the mind runs as a constant explanation machine, trying to form a cohesive story even in the face of improbable information. It's neither good nor bad, simply a neutral mechanism. What have you noticed about your explanation machine?

_____

_____

_____

_____

Contemporary therapies increasingly focus on parts work—the different aspects within one's psyche. As a defusion exercise, imagine your thinking mind is just one part of you. What does it look like, and how does it act? Notice how externalizing your thinking mind can help you to dialogue and defuse.

_____

_____

_____

_____

"Don't believe everything you think" is a saying used in cognitive behavioral therapies. By definition, you believe your beliefs. Instead, treat your thoughts as neutral cognitions rather than assumed fact. Try replacing "I believe . . ." with defusing phrasing, like ". . . is a belief I am holding," at the end of a statement.

_____

_____

_____

_____

Three-Part Grounding into Defusion

You can soothe and defuse. This exercise helps with defusion during high-intensity moments.

1. Notice your thoughts. If you are fused with them, you may feel it as tension, pain, or dissociation.

2. Guide yourself to ground in the body. Your breath may naturally deepen. Notice your physical surroundings.

3. Let go of any struggle against a thought or feeling you are having. Imagine it dissipating into the field around you. You may take an even deeper breath here.

4. Circle back to the challenging thought content. Lightly connect without losing contact with your sense of physical grounding.

5. Whenever it feels like you're starting to fuse or fall in, come back to your breath. Tune into a sense of what is constant and eternal, allowing yourself to connect to your deepest values.

Imagine labeling your thoughts as if you were filing folders. Categorize by form or function. Then file away. Think routine paperwork, easy to handle, and nothing personal. Once you label and file, let it go. Reassure yourself that files will pop up when needed. Reflect on what you notice.

_____

_____

_____

_____

In lucid dreams (when you are dreaming and you realize it's a dream), nightmares can be seen for what they are: unreal and with no power to harm you. Try applying this principle to a troublesome thought. Describe the thought as if it is a bad dream you are observing.

_____

_____

_____

_____

It is possible for you to appreciate the resourcefulness of your thinking even if, as you defuse, you sometimes cringe at it. Remember, you are creating more distance between you and your thoughts, not breaking up with them. How can appreciation for your thinking help you to stay present with a challenging thought?

_____

_____

_____

_____

Get out of your head and into your senses. Ask yourself where the thought is located in your body. Does it have a color, texture, weight? What's underneath it? Notice any impressions or memories that may be connected to the roots of this cognition.

_____

_____

_____

_____

Cognitive Defusion Practice Log

Use this chart as a template to log your cognitive defusion practice. You can use the notes section to record how connected, open, and engaged you felt after practicing the technique. It's okay if you felt otherwise. Simply note your experience.

DATE/TIME	FUSED THOUGHT

COGNITIVE DEFUSION TECHNIQUE	NOTES

How old is the thought? Ask yourself how long you've been having that thought. Maybe it's changed form a bit, but the thought still has the same basic underlying message. Think of the first time you remember having that thought. What was happening? Many thoughts originate in childhood and retain childlike reasoning.

_____

_____

_____

_____

Values can help motivate you to defuse from unhelpful thoughts. Ask yourself how the thought serves you. When you realize a thought does not serve your values, it can be easier to not get hooked into following it.

_____

_____

_____

_____

Think of a time when you completely changed your mind: An enemy turned into a friend, or a scary situation turned out to be funny. Notice how, before you changed your mind, you really believed the opposite was true. Reflecting on such moments can deepen your understanding of defusion.

_____

_____

_____

_____

States of mind can be affected by social contagion, such as the feeling of exhilaration in a festival crowd or the anger of a losing team's fans. This phenomenon helps illustrate the point that we are not our thoughts. As defusion practice, ask yourself "Where did this thought come from?"

_____

_____

_____

_____

Common Fusion Pitfalls

Here are some common patterns of fused thinking. Use the accompanying exercise to notice and nonjudgmentally step outside your fused thoughts—cognitive defusion in action! Keep this list to review when you feel stuck in fusion.

- I get stuck in the "should" zone. I'm upset when things aren't the way they're *supposed* to be.

- I can think of endless reasons why I can't do something. I'm very good at rationalizing my limitations.

- I get weighed down by my judgment of myself and others.

- I often relive the past in reverie or regret.

- My mind is preoccupied with what's going to happen next.

- I tell negative or limiting stories to myself, such as "I'm damaged," or "I don't need anyone."

Fear of losing control of your thoughts can sometimes block efforts to defuse. ACT is about allowing your experience—rather than your thinking mind—to be your guide. Instead of judging control, reflect on your attitude toward controlling your thoughts and the impact of getting into a cycle of control.

_____

_____

_____

_____

Think of a person you admire who rarely seems caught up in their thoughts. When you feel stuck in a particular line of thinking, imagine you are that person. Notice any shifts in relationship to your thoughts. What's different?

_____

_____

_____

_____

I rise above my thoughts, seeing them with appreciation, clarity, and compassion.

Acceptance: Acknowledging the Unpleasant

In ACT, acceptance focuses on allowing your thoughts and emotions to just be, letting go of the struggle against your own inner experience. Acceptance is about making space for both the pleasant and unpleasant, without getting caught up in trying to control, avoid, or eliminate what we don't want to think and feel.

Experiencing uncomfortable emotions, distressing thoughts, painful sensations, or disturbing events is challenging. This can lead to fighting reality through denial, diversion, and other forms of avoidance that are often slippery and not fully in one's awareness. Perhaps it's that you left that self-help book to collect dust on your bookshelf, or that you are avoiding finding a good therapist. It can be subtle and completely internal, like that sense of confusion during tough moments, almost a "does not compute" feeling. ACT sees avoidance as a key component within most psychological suffering. Acceptance is ACT's alternative to avoidance. As you go through the exercises, start by challenging your comfort zone without totally overwhelming yourself. Keep practicing and learning the skill of acceptance before moving on to bigger or more intense situations.

By accepting discomfort,
I am becoming more
resilient, effective,
and wise.

Take a moment to honestly think about where you tend to cling to nonacceptance in relationship to yourself, others, or the world. What would acceptance look like in those relationships?

_____

_____

_____

_____

Sometimes, people resist the concept of acceptance because they think it equals resignation or apathy. Think about how true acceptance is unlike these other states, and how you can tell the difference. Hint: your body can give you signs.

_____

_____

_____

_____

Think about why avoidance leads to suffering and how acceptance works as the healthy alternative to this behavior. Why do you avoid? What is it about the attitude of acceptance that helps you face your fears?

_____

_____

_____

_____

ACT founder Dr. Steven Hayes has said, "If you want it, you can't have it. If you let it go, it's right there." Similarly, I tell my clients, "What you try to get rid of digs in its heels. What you accept transforms." With this in mind, explore the role of paradox in acceptance and how it applies to your life.

_____

_____

_____

_____

Learning to Accept

Take some time to think about what you are learning to accept. Whether they are still aspirational or notions that you have already integrated, review some milestones on your path to greater acceptance.

EXAMPLE: *I am learning to accept that it's human to make mistakes.*

EXAMPLE: *I am learning to accept that it's going to take time to learn these new skills.*

I am learning to accept that

_____ .

I am learning to accept that

_____ .

I am learning to accept that

_____ .

I am learning to accept that

_____ .

I am learning to accept that

_____ .

Treat acceptance as if you were with a shy animal. You can't trick acceptance, pretending to be on its side while secretly coaxing it into a judgment trap. What would it be like to embody the spirit of acceptance toward something you're avoiding, without holding on to conditions or control?

_____

_____

_____

_____

Bring a sense of invitation and curiosity rather than resistance to your suffering. Say you have painful tension in your jaw. You've tried to fix it, but you just tense up more. Instead, be patient, open, and inquisitive; try saying "Welcome, pain in my jaw." Reflect on what you notice.

_____

_____

_____

_____

There may be part of yourself that you wish were different or didn't exist altogether. But trying to eliminate the parts of yourself you dislike will naturally bring up feelings of resistance. How could you approach those parts with neutral or supportive energy?

_____

_____

_____

_____

Sometimes, when you begin to defuse from your thoughts, there can be a lot of judgment. Think about how acceptance can be an antidote to this dilemma. Reflect on a judgment you've made recently about yourself, another person, or a situation. How could you reframe that judgment as acceptance?

_____

_____

_____

_____

Accepting Nonacceptance

This is a mindfulness practice focused on softening and shifting into acceptance. To start, set a timer for five minutes.

1. Find a quiet place and connect with your breath. Feel a sense of expansion on the inhale and grounding on the exhale.

2. Begin observing your inner reality. Practice accepting whatever sensations, thoughts, and emotions come up—pleasant or unpleasant. If judgment or resistance arises, gently acknowledge it without trying to fix or change anything. Keep breathing.

3. Connect with a sense of your deepest yearning. You may feel it in your heart or in other areas. Breathe with the feeling.

4. Notice any blockage to your yearning. What's there? Keep a dual focus on your yearning and the "unacceptable" part, encompassing both with compassionate awareness. See if they want to interact. Be open and curious.

Acceptance is sometimes confused with being so open that you don't have any boundaries. But mindful acceptance involves discernment and grounding in self-care. Think about situations where acceptance and setting firm boundaries go hand in hand.

_____

_____

_____

_____

Some people associate acceptance with weakness or inaction. Think of a situation in which you can accept what is happening while still taking action. What might that look like? Do you see how acceptance and taking action can work together?

_____

_____

_____

_____

When you're feeling sick or exhausted, it can sometimes be easy to feel at peace. That's probably because there is not enough energy in your body and mind to fight reality and reject acceptance! But you can call up this same peaceful state without being under the weather. If you're expending a lot of energy on something without many results, how can you let go of the energy and shift into acceptance?

Forgiveness can help the process of acceptance. Are you holding a grudge against yourself, others, or the world? On the other hand, rushing to forgive can sometimes be avoidance rather than acceptance. Tune into your body to feel if it makes sense for you to practice forgiveness at this time.

Avoidance vs. Acceptance

Let's bring attention to acceptance in the different facets of your life. In each area, mark an "X" where you feel your current level of acceptance is on the scale between avoidance and acceptance. Do you face the tough stuff? Do you run and hide? Or do you do something in between? No judgments—this is about increasing your awareness and accepting yourself wherever you are! Feel free to add other important life areas in the blank categories.

◄ Avoidance   Acceptance ►

Relationship to myself:

Family:

Intimate Relationships:

Work:

Learning/Education:

Social:

_____

_____

Think about something you have trouble accepting. It can be anything from an internal sensation to an external event. As resistance comes up, breathe into a sense of allowing. This doesn't mean you have to like what is happening. Just be with it and breathe. What do you notice?

_____

_____

_____

_____

In quantum theory, a particle and a wave are one thing existing at the same time in two different states. The reality is that there are many different areas of life that dwell within utter contradiction. As humans, it is hard to live within this; sometimes you may feel too polarized to accept, telling yourself that "It can't be this; it *has* to be that." But what will you do when that statement simply isn't true? Write down some ways you can think quantum and practice accepting your life's contradictions.

_____

_____

_____

_____

As unpleasant sensations, feelings, or thoughts come up, note their presence in the simplest terms possible. For example, you could write down "Headache is here," or "Anxiety is present." Let yourself stay with it. If you start thinking it isn't working, note something like "The thought 'This isn't working' is here."

Rather than thinking in all-or-nothing terms—that you either are in acceptance or not—try tuning into the spectrum of your experience. Just notice to whatever degree you are able to be in acceptance. At the same time, allow the part of you that is noticing to soften into acceptance. Reflect on what comes up.

Acceptance Calendar

Feel free to use this calendar to jot down affirmations, note progress in your acceptance process, or plan for situations that may require an extra dose of acceptance.

MONDAY	TUESDAY	WEDNESDAY	THURSDAY
I accept that the beginning of the workweek sometimes feels like a drag.			

FRIDAY	SATURDAY	SUNDAY
Accepting my feelings of annoyance toward TJ.	*Practice acceptance of my sadness about my family's different opinions.*	

Notice how your judgment level goes up and down in any given moment as you take in your surroundings and different thoughts, memories, and impressions arise. You may feel at the mercy of the constant push-pull of aversions and cravings. How can mindful acceptance impact your relationship to this push-pull?

_____

_____

_____

_____

Reassure yourself that what you are experiencing is normal, okay, and possibly even beneficial. For example, try writing "It's normal to not always feel great," "Nobody's perfect," "Everybody has thoughts like that," or, "If I wasn't feeling this pain, I wouldn't understand the changes I need to make."

_____

_____

_____

_____

I am doing the best
that I can, given the
resources available to me
in this very moment.

Contacting the Present: Getting in Touch with the Moment

Alongside acceptance, defusion, and the observing self, contacting the present is a key component of mindfulness in ACT. This process is about "being here now," a phrase that originated with Ram Dass in the 1970s and is often used by best-selling ACT practitioner Russ Harris. In other words, it involves a focused and flexible attention to what is happening—both physically and mentally, within the time and space you find yourself in at any given moment.

It is likely that you spend much of your day thinking about things outside the present. You may be in a state of reverie or rumination over the past. You may be planning for dreading, or looking forward to the future. You may be imagining things that are not right in front of you. This has its purpose, but action only takes place in the present moment. So, to effectively change your life for the better, you want to cultivate presence.

In practice, contacting presence is often achieved via a somatic connection: the breath, sensations, or the senses. Orienting to surroundings is also helpful, particularly natural settings. Physical grounding helps free you from fantasies and past/future thought loops in your head.

I access my power here
and now, in the present
moment.

In busy modern life, it is common for your schedule to feel nonstop. Contacting the present moment is like hopping off the merry-go-round to ground in the here and now. How can this help bring perspective and intentionality to your life choices?

_____

_____

_____

_____

Sati is the original word for mindfulness in Pali, one of the historic languages of Buddhism. It also translates to "remember." Mindful presence is a state you can come back to at any time, simply by remembering to do so. Consider ways to "remember" to come back to presence.

_____

_____

_____

_____

When you deepen your contact with presence, it can feel like waking up to a clearer reality. This is because when you run on mindless autopilot, you're in a less conscious state. Have you ever noticed yourself "wake up" into greater presence? What can you learn from your experience?

_____

_____

_____

_____

Connecting with the body, especially from the neck down, can be an easeful entry point into the present moment. Scan from head to toe, along the spine and limbs. Keep flowing with attention rather than stopping anywhere. What did you notice?

_____

_____

_____

_____

Being Present with Your Emotions

Use this chart to help you meet presence during different emotional states. Consider the "what is needed" column as preparatory conditions to facilitate a shift into greater presence.

STATE:	THOUGHTS/BELIEFS RELATED TO:	WHAT IS NEEDED FOR PRESENCE:
Upset, irritated, angry	"It's not fair." "That's not supposed to happen."	Breathe Body movement (e.g., taking a walk) Acceptance and defusion
Anxious, fearful, avoidant	"It isn't safe." "I can't do it."	Breathe Somatic grounding/seeking safety (e.g., hugging yourself) Invoke boundaries Acceptance and defusion
Overwhelm	"This is too much."	Breathe Physically orient Slow down Acceptance and defusion
Sadness, dejection	"I'm not worthy." "I'm all alone."	Breathe Connecting externally (e.g., being in nature or with animals, inspiring art, kind people) Acceptance and defusion
Joy, excitement, exhilaration	"I feel good." "I'm looking forward to it."	Breathe Somatic grounding

As you emerge into greater presence, you may notice that your breath naturally deepens. You can consciously work with this breath-presence connection. Inhale, expanding your diaphragm so your belly sticks out. Feel your ribs and chest expand. Imagine the breath filling up your head. What do you notice?

_____

_____

_____

_____

It's great that there are apps for mindfulness. Yet increasingly, people rarely sit with their own mind, unguided by someone else's voice. Practice sitting with presence to your thoughts, feelings, and sensations without verbal guidance, music, or even a timer. Reflect on what comes up for you.

_____

_____

_____

_____

Try gently bringing your attention onto one sensory focus. For example, the texture of a surface, the sound of ambient noise, or the flavors while eating with your eyes closed. Stay grounded in your body through your breath. It's okay if this is attentionally challenging. Reflect on what you notice.

_____

_____

_____

_____

You can find presence through nature, away from human distraction. Try going outside and focusing on the natural life around you, even pigeons on a wire or crabgrass along the sidewalk. Don't try to stop your thought streams, emotions, or sensations—just let them be in the background. Reflect on your experience.

_____

_____

_____

_____

Contacting Presence

Take at least five minutes to strengthen your contact with presence. Though the ideal practice is in solitude and relative quiet within nature, know that you can access presence at any time.

1. Connect with your breath. Tell yourself, "I am here now."

2. Slowly take in your surroundings. Lightly sweep your gaze back and forth.

3. Inhale deeply, opening your senses. Feel yourself in your body.

4. Close your eyes to connect with your inner reality.

5. Open your eyes and gently hold awareness of your inner reality alongside the outer world, grounding through your breath.

6. If there is commotion, notice the stillness underneath. If your mind wanders, gently bring it back.

7. Close your eyes again, following your breath to stay connected to the present.

Proprioception is awareness of the movement and position of the body. Using this awareness is called kinesthesia. Try connecting with presence through a kinesthetic sense of balance. Gently sit up in your chair, sit on a yoga ball, or stand on one leg. Notice and reflect on the little corrections the body makes to stay upright.

A 2010 study in *Science* found that people typically spend about half their day outside the present moment, thinking thoughts outside the here and now. Think about the ways you get pulled out of presence. What precipitates and perpetuates these patterns for you?

Contacting presence in the morning can change the frame of your entire day. Especially if you wake up on the proverbial wrong side of the bed! Five minutes of mindful sitting can make a difference. Try it right after you get up. How can this act as a reset?

_____

_____

_____

_____

Contacting presence before sleep can help you feel more rested. Sometimes, you fall asleep because your body is exhausted, but your mind is still wound up. Practicing mindfulness as you prepare to sleep allows your mind to ground and let go. Try following your breath or slowly counting to one hundred. Reflect on your experience.

_____

_____

_____

_____

Challenges to Contacting Presence

Everyone has moments when it's hard to contact presence. List some situations and brainstorm techniques you can use to help.

EXAMPLE: **Challenge to Presence:** It can be hard to contact presence when . . . *I think I've done something wrong.*

Mindful Remedy: I can help myself contact presence by . . . *practicing defusion, acceptance, and grounding.*

EXAMPLE: **Challenge to Presence:** It can be hard to contact presence when . . . *I believe someone is treating me unfairly.*

Mindful Remedy: I can help myself contact presence by . . . *compassionately being with my thoughts and feelings.*

Challenge to Presence: It can be hard to contact presence when . . .

_____

Mindful Remedy: I can help myself contact presence by . . .

_____

Challenge to Presence: It can be hard to contact presence when . . .

_____

Mindful Remedy: I can help myself contact presence by . . .

_____

Many people tend to think of being present as being in solitude. But you can practice presence in relation to another. It's the same formula: Focused and flexible attention grounded in the here and now; accepting thoughts, feelings, and emotions that come up. Explore how presence can enrich your relationships.

_____

_____

_____

_____

Isn't it nice to know that presence is available to you at any time? Try practicing a routine activity with presence; for instance, you could try taking a few deep breaths when you're in line at a shop. Reflect on what you notice.

_____

_____

_____

_____

Your contact with presence can be enhanced through focus on a particular object, such as a seashell, a pebble, a bottle, or whatever is around you. Explore the object through your senses, turn it around in your hand, noticing its properties. Notice the thoughts, feelings, and sensations that come and go.

_____

_____

_____

_____

Sometimes presence is contacted during suffering. You naturally take a deep breath. You tune into details like textures or aromas. Physical grounding liberates you from the mental part of your struggle— when you are trapped in your head and not present. Explore your related experiences.

_____

_____

_____

_____

Mindful Presence—Activity Checklist

Use this checklist to keep track of different ways you can explore coming into contact with presence. Any activity can bring you into presence when done mindfully!

- ☐ Mindful cooking
- ☐ Mindful eating
- ☐ Mindful cleaning
- ☐ Mindful gardening
- ☐ Mindful drawing
- ☐ Mindful walking
- ☐ Mindful grooming

- ☐ Mindful dressing
- ☐ Mindful exercising
- ☐ Mindful external connection (e.g., being with animals, people)
- ☐ Mindful sitting

What other activities can you do with mindful presence?

_____

_____

_____

A frenetic pace can be a sign that you are in a mindless state. You can use this signal to cue yourself to come back into presence. It helps to start by just slowing down what you are doing. What does it feel like to consciously slacken the pace?

_____

_____

_____

_____

Many people love being around animals and babies. One reason may be that these precious nonverbal beings naturally remain in contact with presence. They also tend to feel safer when those around them are also in presence. Explore the interplay between feeling safe and being in contact with presence.

_____

_____

_____

_____

Through my breath,
I connect with presence
whenever I need to.

The Observing Self: Clearly Perceiving Your Thoughts and Feelings

In this chapter, we're going to talk about the observing self. Different than your thinking self, the observing self is the overarching self that witnesses the self that thinks, feels, and does. The observing self can be conceptualized as your higher-level self, an expansive yet grounded presence in which all your experience unfolds.

Important features of the observing self include its constancy, flexibility of attention, and a primarily nonverbal orientation of pure awareness. It can be also likened to a defused self.

In practical terms, the observing self can help you to expand beyond limiting self-concepts. In this way, it can be experienced as stabilizing or transcendent. It might look like a sense of calm washing over you when detaching from an old pattern. Or it may be the feeling of glorious communion while watching a sunrise. The perspective of the observing self can also hold sadness, anxiety, anger, shame, or any other emotion.

In ACT jargon, the observing self is called "self-as-context." Many consider this to be the most esoteric of the six core processes, so know that it's normal to find the concept a bit tricky at first.

I observe and accept
my ever-changing
experience, gaining more
wisdom with each day.

Mindfully sit and let yourself notice how everything changes: thoughts, feelings, sensations. You may feel sleepy, then hot, then irritated, then more clear and accepting. From moment to moment, things change. Reflect on what doesn't change: your observing self. Notice and reflect on what the watcher takes in.

_____

_____

_____

_____

Practice an activity that is easeful and doesn't require much thought, such as coloring in a relaxing coloring book or working with your hands on something physical. Just observe yourself as you go about the process. What do you notice about the self that is thinking, feeling, and doing?

_____

_____

_____

_____

Like a Russian doll in which each figure is nested in a larger version of itself, you can expand your awareness to encompass the previous perspectives. Try practicing this using the following format:

"I am noticing _____ .

Now, I am noticing the one who is noticing _____ ."

_____

_____

_____

_____

Go into nature (or open a window!) and observe plants, animals, and all the other amazing things around you. Look at a line of ants crawling by a tree, watch the clouds moving across the sky, or listen to birds chirping. Note how your observing self is expansive in its identification and its processing of data from outside your psyche. Notice how you feel.

_____

_____

_____

_____

Observing Self and Thinking Self

Review and reflect on this comparative chart, which can serve as a reference guide to distinguish between the observing self and your everyday state of mind. Though you need both states to function in the world, you could likely use more practice shifting to the observing self. Mindful contemplation of the observing self's qualities can be a means of entering into this state of awareness.

THINKING SELF	OBSERVING SELF
Thinking, fused, narrow focus	Pure awareness, expansive, transcendent
Survival, vigilant, problem-solving	Neutrally observant, no agenda
Focus on the past or future	In the present moment
Separate self, ego consciousness	All-encompassing consciousness
Evaluating, judging, critiquing	Compassionate, accepting, nonjudgmental
Moving, chattering, excitable	Stillness, quiet, beyond words, calm
Shifting parts, ever-changing	Constant, ever-present

In fiction, the observing self is like the omniscient narrator to the thinking self's first-person narrator. In omniscient narration, the audience benefits from multiple points of view. What would your "omniscient narrator" say about your current moment?

_____

_____

_____

_____

If the ego is the little you, then the observing self is the big you. Some would say the observing self is closely related to the concept of the "higher self." What are some differences you notice between "little you" and "big you?"

_____

_____

_____

_____

When you watch a movie completely absorbed as if you were experiencing it firsthand, that's like your normal state of the mind—the self that thinks, feels, and does. The observing self is like you in the theater, watching the movie unfold. How does observing your own "movie" change your perspective?

_____

_____

_____

_____

Sometimes you may view the observing self as being devoid of feeling. The observing self does relate to emotion differently, though it is not a robot. As a perspective of pure awareness, it inhabits a more neutral stance toward our emotions. Think of scenarios in which this stance can help.

_____

_____

_____

_____

Mindful Sitting with the Observing Self

This mindfulness exercise promotes connection with your observing self, leading to greater flexibility and perspective.

1. Ground in your felt sense by taking a conscious breath. To deepen the exploration, feel free to close your eyes.

2. Begin to notice your thoughts, feelings, and actions. Notice your train of thought, your emotions, and the movements of your body.

3. Now notice the self that is witnessing the self that is thinking, feeling, and doing. Stay connected with your breath.

4. Continue to ground in your body, tracking sensations and feelings in your overarching awareness. Lightly scan your body, mind, and surroundings without fixating.

5. Notice how you are noticing all these different things at the same time.

6. Notice the one noticing. Keep breathing.

Reflect (literally!) on your observing self: Sit or stand and look in a mirror or use two mirrors at an angle to observe yourself looking at yourself. You may automatically feel judgment. Let that moment pass. Breathe. Compassionately attend to your body language and internal processes. What do you notice?

_____

_____

_____

_____

The concept of the observing self shares similarities with the survival response of dissociation. Both can be experiences of looking from the outside at yourself from a hovering perspective. Yet the former is expansive and the latter restrictive. Explore the distinction between these two categories of experience.

_____

_____

_____

_____

In this breathing exercise, don't try to change your breathing. Don't deepen your breath or consciously control it. Instead, just look at your torso and watch it move with your breath. Let the air breathe into the body. Notice any shifts or insights as you observe.

_____

_____

_____

_____

The observing self is different than the feeling of being scrutinized and judged by a superior presence. Like all ACT processes, it is nonjudgmental and full of ease. Explore how the observing self is different than feeling like someone is watching over your shoulder.

_____

_____

_____

_____

Self-Concept Flexibility

By cultivating the observing self, you can increase flexibility around who you think you can be. Sometimes, you may get too attached to limiting self-concepts. Review this sample list of limiting statements to assess your self-concept flexibility.

- *I think I'm permanently damaged or defective.*

- *I believe that my negative qualities can't be fixed.*

- *I am who I am, and that dictates how I must act.*

- *I punish myself because I know that I'm bad.*

- *Because I'm sick, I can't get better.*

If any of these resonated, it's okay. Though it may still feel like truth, the perspective of the observing self can help free yourself from limiting self-concepts like these.

The goal isn't necessarily to always be in the mode of the observing self. Remember that ACT is ultimately about psychological flexibility, which includes the ability to expand into the perspective of the observing self. How might shifting in and out of this perspective benefit you?

_____

_____

_____

_____

The chessboard is a common ACT metaphor for the observing self. In chess, there are two sides battling it out, representing positive and negative experiences in life. Whichever side wins in any game, the chessboard remains constant, holding all the pieces. Reflect on what's happening on your "chessboard."

_____

_____

_____

_____

Practice shifting into the observing self while relating to another self. This should feel different than how you ordinarily socially monitor yourself. Instead, imagine you are a dispassionate anthropologist from another planet observing the interaction. What do you notice?

_____

_____

_____

_____

In some video games, you can choose between viewing your whole avatar or seeing through your avatar's eyes. In general, the former tends to be easier to navigate whereas the latter can sometimes be disorienting. Reflect on how the whole-avatar perspective can be analogous to the observing self.

_____

_____

_____

_____

Observing Self Worksheet

Using the perspective of the observing self, this worksheet explores how to shift out of limiting self-concepts. You'll also integrate the other core processes of defusion and acceptance while brainstorming more expansive possibilities.

SITUATION	EMOTION	LIMITED SELF-CONCEPT
A falling-out with a friend	Sadness, disappointment, worry	It's my fault, I'm not good enough.

DEFUSION	ACCEPTANCE	NEW POSSIBILITY
These thoughts are older than the friendship.	*I can only do what's in my control. I can breathe in and out with the sadness, disappointment, and worry.*	*I am hopeful for reconciliation and can make space for what arises both internally and externally—whatever the outcome.*

Try having a conversation between your observing self and your everyday self. What's it like to toggle back and forth between these different perspectives? Reflect on what you notice.

_____

_____

_____

_____

The observing self can be likened to the transcendent self, a "pure awareness" that extends to everything, such as when you witness a beautiful sunset, hear a deep poem read aloud, or watch an epic film scene. Recall a transcendent moment. Reflect on your sense of self during that experience.

_____

_____

_____

_____

As I expand my awareness, I expand the possibilities of my identity and existence.

Values: Determining Your Core Motivations

In ACT, values are the guiding principles that motivate you. As ACT founder Steven Hayes has written, values anchor action, acceptance, and defusion into a unified, holistic approach. ACT conceptualizes values as constant and universal. They tend to be abstract and generalizable rather than concrete or exclusive to specific tasks. That way, they're adaptable across different life stages and sectors.

A key ACT exercise involves identifying and ranking your core values. Defining values can sometimes be an emotionally charged process that can activate resistance. Your defense mechanisms may react with avoidance or fusion. Keep in mind those are natural responses. At the same time, sticking with your exploration can lead to feeling greater vibrancy and an expansion of possibilities. It's important to note that values are not what we want or need from others. Clarifying your values is more like an inner dialogue with yourself.

The ACT processes of defining values and committed action are inextricably linked. ACT is a behavioral approach, so the ultimate focus is on effective change in behavior. By first defining your values, you foster movement toward what you truly believe.

Connecting with my values deepens my purpose and meaning.

What do you care about most? What do you feel passionate about? This is one way to identify your values. Remember, you're not thinking about actions just yet. It's about where your heart is, regardless of how close you are to fulfilling that value.

_____

_____

_____

_____

Thinking about people you admire and respect can help you clarify which values mean the most to you. Who are your role models? Why do you look up to them and what do they stand for?

_____

_____

_____

_____

You can deduce your values by thinking about what you don't want. Your values are the reason why you don't want those things. Contemplate the most undesirable labels you can think of, then consider what values are behind your opposition. You may have just found your core values!

_____

_____

_____

_____

Recall times when you felt in the flow, in your element, or at the top of your game—even for just a few moments. Perhaps you felt open, expansive, free. Think back to however you felt. These experiences can be associated with value fulfillment. Explore what values you were connecting with in those moments.

_____

_____

_____

_____

Values Checklist

Circle the values that resonate with you. Rank the top three to five values you identify with. Feel free to add any values not listed here.

☐ Acceptance	☐ Creativity	☐ Meaningfulness
☐ Achievement	☐ Discernment	☐ Nurturance
☐ Adventure	☐ Discipline	☐ Openness
☐ Aesthetics	☐ Discovery	☐ Order
☐ Affection	☐ Diversity	☐ Participation
☐ Authenticity	☐ Ease	☐ Peace
☐ Autonomy	☐ Eclecticism	☐ Peace of mind
☐ Awareness	☐ Effectiveness	☐ Playfulness
☐ Balance	☐ Empathy	☐ Presence
☐ Belonging	☐ Equality	☐ Purpose
☐ Boundaries	☐ Faith	☐ Reciprocity
☐ Celebration	☐ Freedom	☐ Recognition
☐ Challenge	☐ Harmony	☐ Respect
☐ Choice	☐ Honesty	☐ Responsibility
☐ Clarity	☐ Honor	☐ Rigor
☐ Collaboration	☐ Hope	☐ Security
☐ Communication	☐ Humor	☐ Self-expression
☐ Community	☐ Inclusion	☐ Shared reality
☐ Compassion	☐ Independence	☐ Spontaneity
☐ Competence	☐ Inspiration	☐ Stability
☐ Connection	☐ Integrity	☐ Stimulation
☐ Conscientiousness	☐ Intimacy	☐ Strength
☐ Consideration	☐ Joy	☐ Significance
☐ Consistency	☐ Leadership	☐ Trust
☐ Contribution	☐ Learning and growth	☐ Understanding
☐ Cooperation	☐ Love	☐ Warmth

Sometimes when you feel aimless, confused, or ambivalent, it can be that you have not connected with your core values. A common metaphor for values in ACT is your compass—a guidance system for your life's journey. Explore how identifying your deepest-held values can help guide you.

_____

_____

_____

_____

Fears often appear when you home in on your values. You may worry about failing or start to feel overwhelmed. These reactions are normal and can be worked through. Write out some self-compassion affirmations to help reassure you and validate your current state of mind.

_____

_____

_____

_____

Values can be inspirational and aspirational. Imagine you have reached old age, and there is a "This is your life" celebration being thrown for you. What would you want others to say about you? How would you want your life to unfold?

_____

_____

_____

_____

Goals are sometimes mistaken for values. Unlike goals, values cannot be achieved. Even when you reach a goal, the underlying value remains. To uncover the value related to a goal, ask, "Why is accomplishing this goal meaningful to me?" Record your observations.

_____

_____

_____

_____

Heart-Centered Values Exploration

Take some time to mindfully connect with your breath and your somatic awareness.

1. Close your eyes and connect within.

2. Feel into your heart. Observe it through your senses.

3. Step out of your reasoning mind and go abstract. Is there a color, weight, texture, movement? What's around or underneath your heart?

4. Breathe in and out through your heart. Feel into the front, back, and sides of your heart. Notice its spaciousness.

5. Ask your heart, "What do you value most?" Let yourself feel into your heart's aliveness. You may sense a word, an image, or another impression. Even if what you sense doesn't seem to fit your expectations, observe without judgment.

6. Whatever arises, thank your heart for its presence. Be patient and curious about what you discover.

Values exploration can be likened to practices such as meditation, yoga, and tai chi. Though it takes mindful attention and effort, there can be a big payoff. You may develop greater trust in yourself, or you may feel more self-assured. What benefits do you anticipate from exploring your values?

_____

_____

_____

_____

Feelings are sometimes confused with values. The concepts are different but related. Your values can power your feelings. Values are so important that even when you subjectively feel terrible, you can still find peace when you are value aligned. Reflect on the relationship between values and your feelings.

_____

_____

_____

_____

Connection with your values can help you through tough moments. It can help you defuse from the immediacy of something unpleasant and look at the big picture. Doing so also helps with acceptance. Think about a time when your values helped you persist through a challenging situation.

_____

_____

_____

_____

Though values are constant, your relationship to a value can change. That's part of psychological flexibility. In ACT, you prioritize your values in the here and now. But values aren't like a change of clothes—they tend to be consistent within a stage of life. Reflect on this balance.

_____

_____

_____

_____

Connection to Your Values

Take time to assess your connection to your values. Rate the following statements from zero (strongly disagree) to five (strongly agree).

I know what I stand for. _____

I've consciously chosen what's most important in my life. _____

My values can be different from other people's. _____

My core values are adaptable and can evolve. _____

I prioritize my values. _____

My values guide me. _____

SCORE: _____

0 to 10   A good start on your values journey

10 to 20   A solid foundation in your values exploration

20 to 30   A grounded and strong sense of your values

Connecting with your values can sometimes be upsetting, especially if you feel disconnected from them in your daily life. Imagine lifting a rug and realizing it had bugs underneath. Initially, you may feel bad. But only through awareness can you make things better. How can practicing acceptance help?

_____

_____

_____

_____

What if, instead of the common question, "What do you want to be when you grow up?" children were asked, "What are your values?" The great thing about values is their adaptability. Different professions, roles, and lifestyles can reflect the same underlying value. Think about what values your childhood aspirations reflected.

_____

_____

_____

_____

Connecting with your values in your daily life can help you stay motivated, present, and enthusiastic. But sometimes, feelings of apathy, mindlessness, and lethargy can come up. Often, this is a sign that your defense mechanisms have activated. Consider how defusion can help you stay engaged with the process.

_____

_____

_____

_____

Values discussions can get a bad rap when mistakenly associated with dogma or intolerance. And sometimes, you're taught that everything is relative, so it's pointless to think about values. But everyone has values—that's what makes life meaningful. Explore how you can reclaim the values conversation for yourself.

_____

_____

_____

_____

Values in Your Life Arenas

Write out what is most important to you within these different arenas and aspects of your life. Then examine your statements and drill down to the underlying values.

INTIMATE PARTNERSHIPS:

What is most important to you? _____

Underlying values: _____

FAMILY:

What is most important to you? _____

Underlying values: _____

WORK:

What is most important to you? _____

Underlying values: _____

FRIENDSHIPS:

What is most important to you? _____

Underlying values: _____

COMMUNITY:

What is most important to you? _____

Underlying values: _____

CREATIVITY:

What is most important to you? _____

Underlying values: _____

HEALTH/PHYSICAL:

What is most important to you? _____

Underlying values: _____

INTELLECTUAL/MENTAL:

What is most important to you? _____

Underlying values: _____

PASSIONS/INTERESTS:

What is most important to you? _____

Underlying values: _____

SPIRITUAL/RELIGIOUS:

What is most important to you? _____

Underlying values: _____

OTHER:

What is most important to you? _____

Underlying values: _____

It may be the case that you automatically adopted the values of your environment: society, peer group, loved ones. Ultimately, this may or may not resonate with your true values. Consider how you can continue to make room for authentic values exploration, even in the face of others' judgment.

_____

_____

_____

_____

Awareness of your values can help build communities of affinity and draw more meaningful relationships into your life. Embracing your core values creates opportunities to connect with like-minded folks and nourish your soul within the experience of collective vision. Let yourself imagine the possibilities!

_____

_____

_____

_____

My values keep me
steady on my life's
journey.

Committed Action: Doing What Matters to You

As a behavioral approach, ACT is interested in practical results. As such, all the ACT core processes circle back to committed action as the end goal. If you stopped at defining values, you would not have fulfilled the work you have started. Action is necessary to complete the steps.

In ACT, committed action is values-based action that moves you toward fulfillment of values-based goals. This action takes place in the real world, even in the face of obstacles. Other ACT processes—especially acceptance and defusion—are vital tools to address any obstacles that may arise.

Committed action is a concrete and task-oriented process. The process builds on itself, so that the steps involved can become larger and more complex the further into it you get. Flexibility is an important quality. Objectives are most effective when they are specific, measurable, time based, and realistic. An optimal action plan balances accountability with permission to tweak the process as you go along.

I commit to action based
on my values.

If you were granted a magic wish to make your life exactly as you want it to be, what would it look like? Now think of the first step to take along the way. Let it be bite-size. Remember defusion and acceptance can help you unblock. Explore your reaction.

_____

_____

_____

_____

The idea of committed action may sound overwhelming at first. To get started, it can help to chunk it down into manageable steps—things that are immediately actionable. The point is to compassionately meet yourself where you're at. Brainstorm one baby step you can take to align closer to your values.

_____

_____

_____

_____

Detours are normal on your committed action journey. Values are your trusty compass. But don't cling to the compass, afraid to take a step without staring at it. Instead, return to it as needed, building confidence in your innate ability to navigate. Reflect on this values-to-action balance.

_____

_____

_____

_____

Committed action is mindful action. Basing your action on your chosen values is vital. So is staying connected to present moment awareness. Somatic attunement is an easily accessible means of contacting presence. Brainstorm one committed action you could take and plan to do so mindfully.

_____

_____

_____

_____

Generative Inspiration for Committed Action

This checklist of generative activities can act as inspiration for committed action.

The idea is to use these as values-directed activities that help you get started in moving closer toward your values-guided goals as quickly and effectively as possible. Take five minutes to engage in one small action toward one of the items you've checked off here.

CREATIVE INSPIRATION:

- ☐ Vision board
- ☐ Songs/playlist
- ☐ Poems, books
- ☐ Performance art
- ☐ Arts and crafts
- ☐ Journaling

INTENSIVES:

- ☐ Meditation retreat
- ☐ Time in nature
- ☐ Personal growth workshop
- ☐ Education course
- ☐ Ritual or ceremony
- ☐ Travel or journeys

SHARED REALITY WITH OTHERS:

- ☐ Advice from role models/mentorship
- ☐ Like-minded peers
- ☐ Communal gathering/ networking

When your values are off target, it can lead to a seeming lack of motivation for committed action. It could be that you're taking on other people's values or that your values date to a past stage of your life. Consider why authentic values alignment is so important for committed action.

The goals you set as part of your committed action plan are most effective when held with flexibility and a sense of self-trust. Reflect on what happens when you set goals that are too rigid or when you don't trust yourself to achieve your goals.

Ideal goals are adaptable, practical, and measurable. Though opinions may vary on what exactly is "realistic," your goal should be achievable. Based on these parameters, how can you optimize your goals?

_____

_____

_____

_____

Committed action reflects an essential choice of life. This choice is not about whether to feel pain or not—painful moments are simply an aspect of being alive. Rather, it's about the choice of living a values-based life or not. Reflect on this idea.

_____

_____

_____

_____

Committed Action Plan

Set aside some time to develop a plan for taking action.

1. Formulate a values-based goal.

2. Break down the goal into discrete steps.

3. Make the first step immediately actionable. It can be a symbolic gesture, but must involve real-life action. For example, writing up a to-do list.

4. Move through the steps. If you feel lost or overwhelmed, practice mindfulness to stay connected, open, and engaged. Then, reconnect with the underlying values. If need be, chunk down the next step into even smaller actions of less duration or effort.

5. When faced by roadblocks, make use of defusion, acceptance, presence, and the observing self.

6. Debrief on what values you moved closer to.

You can prepare to confront obstacles as you work toward committed action. Managing expectations is half the battle because it's pretty typical for avoidance and unhelpful thoughts to come up as part of the process. How can you reframe your experience when resistance comes up?

_____

_____

_____

_____

Self-compassion—being kind and understanding toward yourself in the face of perceived inadequacy or suffering—is a proven method for enhancing performance. Motivation works better with the promise of a carrot rather than the threat of a stick. How can you apply self-compassion as you work on committed action?

_____

_____

_____

_____

In general, you likely want to focus on what you want rather than what you don't want. But it can be helpful to acknowledge the price you would pay if you didn't choose committed action. What would you be missing out on? Are you willing to pay that price?

Get organized to help take committed action. Use reminders, a calendar planner, and schedule self-reviews to keep yourself on track. Brainstorm organizational tricks to help with accountability. Start practicing and note what works best for you. Give yourself room to experiment. Trial and error are part of the process.

_____

_____

_____

_____

_____

_____

_____

_____

_____

_____

_____

_____

Committed Action Worksheet

Use this worksheet to get real-world practice in committed action. Think of the Big Picture as the overarching goal. The Action is what you will do to get to the Big Picture. And the First Step is the initial move you need to make within the Action. Break down the first step into manageable tasks and begin with the first one right away.

SITUATION	VALUES	BIG PICTURE
I want to change jobs.	Security Learning Adventure	Work as a consultant.
I'm not sure if I want kids.	Freedom Connection Love	I want to be sure of my decision either way.
I'm at risk for diabetes.	Longevity Stability Independence	Maintain my health.

ACTION	FIRST STEP	NOTES
Pursue a business degree.	*Research grad schools online.*	*Created list of potential schools.*
Get more experience being around children.	*Call up friends with kids.*	
Improve my overall wellness.	*Reduce sugar intake and increase activity.*	

Be on the lookout for "Just say no" habitual responses. It's okay to be afraid when faced with things you want to accomplish. Yearning involves vulnerability. Your defenses can show up as reflexive reason giving that resists committed action. How can acceptance and defusion soften the edges around these responses?

_____

_____

_____

_____

No one is an island unto themselves. You can reinforce support for committed action by introducing the topic in friendly conversation or sharing your goals with trusted confidants. Explore what comes up for you when considering enlisting others in this way.

_____

_____

_____

_____

Healthy skepticism is perfectly fine. Any process or relationship should earn your trust over repeated experiences. At the same time, you need to cultivate a willingness to try. Explore how you can encourage an attitude of willingness and openness to the practice of committed action.

_____

_____

_____

_____

Like academic studies or a fitness program, committed action involves work. But you can also feel a joyful flow. The flow state hits a sweet spot where ability and effort are Goldilocks-level challenging—just the right amount to keep you interested but not overly stressed. Explore crafting Goldilocks-inspired goals.

_____

_____

_____

_____

_____

_____

Compassion toward Committed Action Blockage

ACT expert Russ Harris utilizes the following helpful acronyms to remove obstacles to committed action.

From **F.E.A.R.** to **D.A.R.E.**:

F	Fusion	D	Defusion
E	Excessive goals	A	Acceptance of discomfort
A	Avoidance of discomfort	R	Realistic goals
R	Remoteness from values	E	Embracing values

EXAMPLE: *If I join a gym, I'll realize that I'm lazy.*

F	Unhelpful thoughts: "I'm lazy"	D	"I'm having the thought that I'm lazy."
E	Intimidated by fitness celebrities	A	It's normal to have fears around exercise.
A	Procrastinate	R	I take smaller steps like a day pass.
R	Forget my reasons	E	My value of balance motivates me.

Now try your own:

F_____

E_____

A_____

R_____

D _____

A_____

R_____

E_____

Just as in the addiction recovery model, "relapse" can be framed as a built-in expectation. That is, broken commitments are part of what it means to be human. Explore your attitude toward making mistakes or falling short. Consider the role of acceptance and other ACT core processes.

_____

_____

_____

_____

_____

As ACT founder Steven Hayes has written, once you progress further into the process, you will find that successively larger patterns of committed action are necessary. These keep the momentum and sustain the path toward your goals. Explore how a values-based, step-by-step approach can facilitate expansion into larger patterns of action.

_____

_____

_____

_____

_____

I am moving closer to
a rich and meaningful
life through
committed action.

A FINAL NOTE

Congratulations—you made it to the finish line! Completing this book took dedication and real effort. Pat yourself on the back for a job well done. If you made it this far, your persistence and commitment demonstrate that you are well on your way.

Hopefully, your hard work has translated into responding to your stressors in a way that's more aligned with your values. Years from now, you may even look back on this time as a pivotal moment in your development. But please don't see this as the end of your ACT journey. Really, it's just the beginning.

RESOURCES

Books

The Happiness Trap by Russ Harris (Wollombi, NSW, Australia: Exisle Publishing, 2007). This international bestseller is one of the most widely used ACT self-help books.

Acceptance and Commitment Therapy, Second Edition: The Process and Practice of Mindful Change by Steven Hayes, Kirk Strosahl, and Kelly Wilson (New York: Guilford Press, 2016). This seminal textbook by the originators of ACT comprehensively covers its principles, research into its effectiveness, and its clinical applications.

Websites

A global directory of ACT-trained therapists may be found through the Association for Contextual Behavioral Science (ACBS): ContextualScience.org.

I recommend the Audible course by ACT founder Steven Hayes, PhD, titled "Principles to Overcome Negativity, Become More Effective, and Transform Your Life," available on his website: StevenCHayes.com /soundstrue.

I also recommend Hayes's TEDx Talk, "Psychological Flexibility: How Love Turns Pain into Purpose," YouTube.com/watch?v=o79_gmO5ppg.

Steven Hayes's ACT-related blog: StevenCHayes.com/blog.

In-person and online workshops with renowned ACT trainer Russ Harris, MD: ActMindfully.com.au.

Judy Ho, PhD, her quick intro video to ACT: YouTube.com/watch?v=LLjzGVCM8ik.

Dr. Ho's 25-minute demonstration of an ACT therapy session: YouTube.com/watch?v=HklLoSB8iso.

Podcasts

I recommend a podcast by Diana Hill, PhD, *Welcome to Your Life in Process Podcast: Psychological Flexibility from the Inside Out*, available on all streaming services.

REFERENCES

Barnard, Laura K., and John F. Curry. "Self-Compassion: Conceptualizations, Correlates, & Interventions." *Review of General Psychology* 15, no. 4 (December 2011): 289–303. doi: 10.1037/a0025754.

Cushman, Fiery. "Rationalization Is Rational." *Behavioral and Brain Sciences* 43 (2020): e28. doi: 10.1017/S0140525X19001730.

Dass, Ram. 1971. *Be Here Now, Remember*. San Cristobal, NM: Lama Foundation.

Harris, Russ. *ACT Made Simple: A Quick Start Guide to ACT Basics and Beyond*. Oakland, CA: New Harbinger, 2009.

_____. *The Happiness Trap: Stop Struggling, Start Living*. Wollombi, NSW, Australia: Exisle Publishing, 2007.

Hayes, S. C. "Acceptance and Commitment Therapy, Relational Frame Theory, and the Third Wave of Behavioral and Cognitive Therapies." *Behavior Therapy* 35 (2004): 639–665. doi: 10.1016/S0005-7894(04)80013-3.

Hayes, Steven, Kirk Strosahl, and Kelly Wilson. *Acceptance and Commitment Therapy, Second Edition: The Process and Practice of Mindful Change*. New York: Guilford Press, 2016.

Hayes, S. C., K. W. Wilson, E. V. Gifford, V. M. Follette, and K. Strosahl. "Experiential Avoidance and Behavioral Disorders: A Functional Dimensional Approach to Diagnosis and Treatment." *Journal of Consulting and Clinical Psychology* 64 (1996). doi: 10.1037/0022-006X.64.6.1152.

Killingsworth, M. A., and D. T. Gilbert. "A Wandering Mind Is an Unhappy Mind." *Science* 330 (2010): 932. doi: 10.1126/science.1192439.

Acknowledgments

Thank you to my spouse and life partner, C. Erik Sayle, for the strength of your loving support throughout the years. Thanks to my sister, Lisa Herrmann, for encouraging me to keep working toward my lifelong goal of book authorship. Thanks, Mom and Dad!

Gratitude for Dr. Stephen Gilligan, for your brilliance and compassionate mentorship. And Dr. Phyllis Grilikhes-Maxwell, creative writer and psychologist, for inspiring me to follow the same path. Special thanks to Callisto editors Rakhshan Rizwann and Olivia Bartz for believing in me.

Thank you Universe, Ancestors, Higher Self, Goddess, and Mother Earth.

About the Author

Josie Valderrama, PsyD, is a licensed clinical psychologist based in San Francisco. Her focus encompasses ethical non-monogamy, anxiety, spirituality, and working with fellow LGBTQ+ people and people of color. As a researcher, Dr. Valderrama created a novel problematic smartphone use scale. She contributed as a subject matter expert to the 2022 revision of the California Psychology Law and Ethics Examination. Dr. Valderrama is a founding member of Bay Area Open Minds, a therapist network affirming sexual and gender diversity. She mentors and supervises future colleagues at the Liberation Institute. In addition to ACT, Dr. Valderrama draws upon feminist, multicultural, and trancework approaches.

CPSIA information can be obtained
at www.ICGtesting.com
Printed in the USA
BVHW020123150522
637041BV00027B/304

9 781638 787464